EARLY 60s FASHION STYLE

✱ ✱ ✱

EARLY 60's FASHION STYLE

Copyright © 2003 P I E BOOKS

All rights reserved. No part of this publication may be reproduced in
any form or by any means, graphic, electronic or mechanical,
including photocopying and recording by an information storage and
retrieval system, without permission in writing from the publisher.

P I E BOOKS
2-32-4, Minami-Otsuka, Toshima-ku,
Tokyo 170-0005 Japan
Tel:+81-3-5395-4811 Fax:+81-3-5395-4812

http://www.piebooks.com
e-mail：editor@piebooks.com
　　　　sales@piebooks.com

ISBN4-89444-306-6 C0070
Printed in Japan

CONTENTS

- 8 Light and cheery
- 26 Beach bunny
- 50 summer
- 74 Popsicle brights
- 94 World traveler
- 118 Sophisticates
- 132 winter
- 148 Coats
- 162 Indoors
- 182 Hairdos
- 194 Shoes
- EARLY 60's FASHION STYLE

PREFACE

EARLY 60's (1960-1965)

fashion director :
清水早苗/Sanae Shimizu
translator : Pamela Miki

「The Swinging Sixties」、社会的にも性においても自由が広がった60年代は、服飾史上、大変革期と定義づけられている。

第二次世界大戦によって、大打撃を受けたパリ・モード。その復権に貢献したのはクリスチャン・ディオールだった。戦後の女性の服装は、ミリタリー調の肩の張ったジャケットと膝下丈のスカートが一般的で、戦時中の影響が続いていた。そういう時期に、ディオールが、1947年に発表した、女性の身体の線を優しく描き出したエレガントなシルエットは、戦争を経験し、実用的な服に流れていた女性達の心をまたたく間につかみ、「ニュー・ルック」と呼ばれた。ディオールは、大成功をおさめた後も、新しいラインを次々と発表し、パリ・モードの世界的な影響を決定づけた。50年代、オート・クチュールはバレンシアガ、ディオール、ジバンシー、ランバンといった偉大なクチュリエ達が活躍する絶頂期を迎えることになる。
50年代後半は、戦後の復興期であり、先進国は驚異的な高度成長を遂げていた。それに伴って生まれてきた中産階級。そして、戦争直後の空前のベビーブーム。欧米の階級社会がゆらぎはじめていた。上流階級主導のモードに対する若者の反発が、社会現象として顕在化してくるのは、62、3年頃からであり、それまでは、一般的な人々の服装は、50年代後半の雰囲気が続いていた。

クリストバル・バレンシアガとサック・ドレス

クリスチャン・ディオールをして、「我々クチュリエは、オート・クチュールの楽士のようなもので、バレンシアガというコンダクターの指揮に従っている」と言わしめたバレンシアガは、まさにオート・クチュールの巨匠達のなかの巨匠。厳密なカットと縫製技術によって、革新的なフォルムを相次いで発表していった。40年代後半からはじまった、マヌカンのような完璧な身体を持たない女性達のための、身体に密着しない新しいドレスの構築への試みは、55年のチュニック・ドレス、57年のサック・ドレスを生み出した。特に、ウエストに切り替えのないチューブ形のサック・ドレスは、「ニュー・ルック」に変わり、多くのデザイナー達に影響を与えた。サックとは、袋という意味。また、そのシンプルなパターンは、プレタポルテ産業が発展する重要な要因となり、60年代のミニ・ドレスを予見するものと評価されている。ちなみに、65年にミニ・スカートを発表したアンドレ・クレージュは、50年代、バレンシアガのもとで、11年間働いていた。60年代の初頭、「ハーパース・バザー」誌の編集長は、「今日全ての女性は、なんらかの形でバレンシアガを着ている」と記述している。

ビート・ジェネレーション

50年代中頃、アメリカに、「ビートニク」あるいは、「ビート族」とよばれる若者達が現れた。自らをビート・ジェネレーション（うちひしがれた世代）と呼び、物質文明に疑問を投げかけ、精神性を求める知的な若者達だ。彼らは、労働者の作業着である革のジャンパーとブルージーンズを着て、自らの生き方を表現した。ビートニクは、ヨーロッパへも多大な影響をもたらすが、はじめの頃は、思想ではなく、表層的なファッションとして伝わり、社会からドロップアウトした暴力集団の若者に取り入れられた。
この頃、パリでは、「実存主義者」（エグジスタンシャリスト）と呼ばれる、哲学者サルトルの影響を受けた若者達が、黒のプルオーバーと細身のパンツを着て、サンジェルマン・デ・プレ界隈に現れていた。
やがて、ビートニク現象を通じて、革ジャンとブルージーンズ、Tシャツが、次第に世界中の若者の新しいファッションとして広まっていく。これは、階級社会に対応したオート・クチュール中心の流れとは全く異なる、自然発生的なストリート・ファッションの登場だった。

モッズ

モダーンズの略語であるモッズは、50年代のモダン・ジャズ・ファンにさかのぼる。当初、未来派のスタイルを目指したモッズは、仕立ての良いテーラードスーツが基本だった。60年代初め、ロンドンのカーナビーストリートを中心に、世界的に流行した、モッズ・スタイルが風俗として注目されはじめる頃には、モッズキャップとよばれる船員帽、ミリタリー長のジャケット、花柄や水玉プリントのシャツ、股上の浅いパンツといった独特のスタイルをつくりあげた。60年代末におこる、男性がカラフルに着飾るピーコック革命の先駆けとなった。

プレタポルテの誕生

既製服産業は、19世紀末、イギリスとアメリカで始まったといわれている。当初は、「コンフェクション」と呼ばれ、安物の既製服のことを意味していた。ドイツ、ベルリンでは、すでにクチュールに近い縫製技術をもった、高級既製服の製造業者が現れていたが、ベルリンを分断する壁の設置によって、衰退を余儀なくされた。戦後の、何でも売れた「買走り」の時代を経て、消費者は次第に、質と流行に目を向けるようになっていく。安物のイメージがぬぐいきれない「コンフェクション」という言葉に変わって、新しい既製服の呼び名が求められ、「プレタポルテ」という言葉が生まれた。初めて使われたのは、1949年。英語のready to wearを、そのままフランス語にしたものだった。50年代のプレタポルテは、流行を左右していたオート・クチュールのデザインを焼き直し、消費者に広めていたに留まっていた。60年代に入ってから、スチリストと呼ばれるプレタポルテ企業のデザイナー達が、独自のコレクションを発表しはじめ、プレタポルテは産業として飛躍的な発展を遂げて行く。オート・クチュールのデザイナーのなかでも、いち早く、ピエール・カルダンとイヴ・サンローランは、中流階級のためのプレタポルテ部門を開設し、敏感に時代の波に対応していった。

ファッションリーダー

ファッションの情報源は、もはや、ファッション雑誌やジャーナリストだけではなくなった。ミュージシャンや映画スターが若者達のファッションへ影響をもたらすようになる。ロックのアイドル、エルビス・プレスリーがビートニクを、初期のビートルズはモッズを代表した。また、女優・オードリー・ヘップバーンと最後のクチュリエと呼ばれるユベール・ド・ジバンシーの関係も特筆に値する。映画「麗しのサブリナ」以来、一貫してヘップバーンの衣装を担当してきたジバンシー。その時々の先端のファッションが、銀幕の中で見事に着こなすヘップバーンを通して、観客に伝わっていった。そして、故ジョン・F・ケネディ大統領のファースト・レディとして活躍していた時のジャクリーヌ・ケネディ。彼女も世界中の女性から注目を浴び、そのコスチュームが常に話題を呼んだ。

60年代前期は、戦後の経済成長によって生まれた中産階級と、ベビーブーマー世代のパワーによって、欧米の階級社会が崩れつつある時期だった。それにともなう顧客の変化によって、オート・クチュールの経営自体も困難になってくる。上流階級から大衆へという構図が崩れ、ファッションの担い手が、若者、そして大衆へと移行していく過渡期だった。

参考文献：
「パリモードの200年 II」南静著　文化出版
「世界服飾史」深井晃子監修　美術出版社
「20世紀モード史」ブリュノ・デュ・ロゼル著／西村愛子訳　平凡社
「FASHION OF A DECADE THE 1960s」Yvonne Connikie著　B.T.Batsford Ltd
「BALENCIAGA」原文　マリ・アンドレ・ジューヴ、ジャクリーヌ・ドモルネックス
日本版監修　上田安子　学校法人　上田学園

"The Swinging Sixties" — the decade of expanded social and sexual freedom is defined as the period that reshaped fashion history.

With World War II, Paris mode suffered a severe blow, and Christian Dior contributed greatly to its restoration. Postwar women's clothing continued to reflect the influence of the war years, with jackets sporting military-style shoulders and hems below the knee the norm. Presented in 1947, Dior's elegant silhouette, gently drawing out the lines of the body, immediately captured the hearts of those women who had suffered through the war in their practical clothes, coming to be known as the "New Look." Dior followed upon this success with new line after new line, cementing the global influence of Paris fashion. In the 50s, haute couture would see its golden age, with legendary couturiers such as Balenciaga, Dior, Givenchy and Lanvin active.

In the latter half of the decade, as the world recovered from the war, the developed world experienced spectacular growth. This period also saw the rise of the middle class, as well as an unprecedented "baby boom" after the war. The social strata of Europe and America began to crumble. By 1962 or 63 the rejection by the young of the fashion of the rich would be a social phenomenon, but until that time the clothes worn by the average person continued in the same style as the 50s.

Cristobal Balenciaga and the "Sack Dress"

Balenciaga was a giant among the giants of haute couture; Christian Dior once said, "We couturiers are like musicians, following the direction of Balenciaga the conductor." With precise cutting and sewing technique, he produced revolutionary designs one after another. His experiments, beginning in the late 40s, in designing dresses for those women not blessed with perfect, mannequin-like figures resulted in 1955's "Tunic Dress" and 1957's "Sack Dress." In particular, the tube-shaped, waistless Sack Dress changed the New Look, influencing a great many designers. In addition, the simple design was an essential element for the development of pret-a-porter manufacturing. The design can also be appreciated as a precursor to the mini-skirt of the 60s. Incidentally, the man who developed the mini-skirt in the early 60s, Andre Courreges, worked as an apprentice of Balenciaga's in the 50s. In the early 60s the editor of Harper's Bazaar wrote, "Today, in one form or another, every woman is wearing Balenciaga."

The Beat Generation

In the 1950s in America, a group of young people calling themselves Beatniks, or the Beat (as in "beat down") Generation, appeared. Intelligent young people, they raised doubts about the culture of material possession and sought spirituality. They wore the leather jackets and blue jeans that were the uniform of the workers, as an expression of their concept of how one should live. The Beatniks would heavily influence Europe, but at first the influence was superficial rather than ideological, as gangs of young social dropouts adopted their fashion. About that time in Paris, the "Existentialists," a movement of young philosophers heavily influenced by Sartre, appeared in the area of Saint Germain-du-Pre, wearing black pullovers and tight-fitting pants.

In time, through the Beatnik phenomenon, the leather jumper, blue jeans and t-shirt would gradually become the fashion for youngsters around the world. This was entirely separate from the developments in haute couture, which was created for a class society — it was the natural, spontaneous appearance of a "street fashion."

The Mods

The Mods (a contraction of the word "Moderns") can be traced back to the fans of "modern jazz" in the 1950s. In their early years they sought a futuristic style, with the basic uniform a well-tailored suit. At the beginning of the 1960s, the fashion, centered on London's Carnaby Street, came in vogue around the world. When the Mods style first began to gain attention as a fashion, the sailor cap known as the "mod cap," military style jackets, floral or polka-dot print shirts and low-waisted pants formed the mainstays of this unique style. In it we can see foreshadowed the colorful male dress of the "peacock revolution" that would follow in the 60s.

The Birth of Pret-a-porter

The ready-made fashion industry is said to have begun in the late 19th century in England and America. Called "confection" in its early years, it meant cheap, pre-made clothing. In Berlin, Germany, there appeared a community of seamstresses and tailors producing high-quality ready-made clothing at very close to the couture level, but after the construction of the Berlin Wall the industry's decline was inevitable. After the "buy-and-run" era of the postwar years when anything would sell, consumers gradually began to pay closer attention to elements such as quality and fashion. Searching for a replacement for the "confection" label and its irreparable aura of cheapness, marketers conceived the term "pret-a-porter."

The word, a direct translation into French of the English "ready to wear," was first used in 1949. Pret-a-porter fashion in the 1950s did little more than rehash the haute couture designs that held sway over fashion. In the 1960s, pret-a-porter designers began to develop their own fashion lines, and pret-a-porter as an industry began to grow rapidly. Even haute couture designers, the first being Pierre Cardin and Yves St. Laurent, established pret-a-porter lines aimed at the middle class, keenly responding to the wave of the times.

Fashion Leaders

Sources of information on fashion were no longer limited to fashion magazines and reporters. Musicians and movie stars influenced the fashion of young people. Among rock idols, Elvis Presley represented Beatnik fashion, while the Beatles represented the Mods. As well, special mention should be made of the relationship between Audrey Hepburn and Hubert de Givenchy, called the last of the couturiers. From the film "Sabrina" on, Givenchy was responsible for all of Audrey Hepburn's clothing. This often avant-garde style was transferred through the stylish image of Audrey Hepburn on the silver screen to the viewer. Jacqueline Kennedy, as she was known when she was First Lady to the late President John F. Kennedy, was also looked to as a fashion leader by women around the world, her costume always a topic of conversation.

The first half of the 1960's were a time of change, as the middle class, born from post-war economic growth, and the power of the Baby Boom generation contributed to the collapse of class society in Europe and America. At the same time, changes in the consumer class caused problems for the haute couture system itself. The flow of fashion from the upper classes to the proletariat was replaced in this transitional period by transmission from fashion leader, to youth, to the masses.

References
Connickie, Yvonne. "Fashions of a Decade: The 1960s". (BT Batsford Ltd).
Du Roselle, Bruno. "La Mode". (Paris: Imprimerie Nationale, 1980).
Translated by Aiko Nishimura under the title "20 seiki modo shi" (Heibonsha, 1995).
Fukai, Akiko. "Sekai fukushoku shi". (Bijustsu shuppansha, 1998).
Jouve, Marie-Andre, and Jacqueline Demornex. "Balenciaga". (London: Thames and Hudson, 1989).
Translated under the supervision of Yasuko Uedo (Ueda Gakuen).
Minami, Shizuka. "Pari modo no 200 nen II". (Bunkashuppan, 1990).

CHRONOLOGICAL TABLE

1960
- ディオールの後継者、イヴ・サンローランが徴兵されマルク・ボアンがアート・ディレクター代理に就任
- カラー・テレビの本放送始まる

1961
- イヴ・サンローラン 独立
- アンドレ・クレージュ パリにメゾン開店
- ジョン・F・ケネディ 米大統領に就任
- ソ連、有人宇宙飛行成功
- ベルリンの壁が作られる

1962
- ニューヨークでアメリカ・ファッション・デザイナーズ協議会発足
- マリー・クワントがミニ・スカート発表
- サンローラン メゾン創設 ファースト・コレクション発表
- 米、有人宇宙飛行成功
- キューバ危機
- ビートルズ、ローリング・ストーンズデビュー

1963
- パンティ・ストッキング発表
- マリー・クワント、ジンジャーグループをスタートさせる
- アンドレ・クレージュ、「パンツ・ルック」を発表
- ケネディ大統領暗殺
- イギリスでビートルズ人気が社会現象となり、「ビートルマニア」という言葉が生まれる

1964
- ルディ・ガーンライヒ、トップレス水着を発表
- ジェフリー・ビーン会社を設立
- ピエール・カルダン、「スペースエッジ」ファッションを発表
- ブティック「ビバ」、ロンドンに開店
- ビートルズ、アメリカに上陸
- 東京オリンピック開催

1965
- アンドレ・クレージュ、65春夏オートクチュールで「ミニ・スカート」を発表
- イヴ・サンローラン、「モンドリアン・ドレス」を発表
- オプ・アート、ポップ・アートの影響
- アメリカ空軍の北ベトナム爆撃開始
- 日韓基本条約調印、国交回復

1960
- Dior successor Yves Saint Laurent is drafted; Marc Bohan takes over as art director
- Color television broadcasting begins

1961
- Yves Saint Laurent goes out on his own
- Andre Courreges opens his own house in Paris
- John F. Kennedy becomes president of the United States
- Soviet cosmonaut safely orbits and returns to Earth
- Berlin Wall is built

1962
- Council of Fashion Designers of America founded in New York
- Mary Quant launches the mini skirt
- Yves Saint Laurent opens his own house and shows his first collection
- US astronaut safely orbits and returns to Earth
- Cuban Missile Crisis
- The Beatles and The Rolling Stones make their debuts

1963
- Pantyhose came on the market
- Mary Quant sets up the Ginger Group
- Andre Courreges introduces the pants look
- President John F. Kennedy assassinated
- The Beatles' popularity becomes a social phenomenon the term "Beatlemania" is coined

1964
- Rudi Gernreich introduces the topless bathing suit
- Geoffrey Beene forms his own company
- Pierre Cardin introduces "Space-age" fashion
- Boutique Biba opens in London
- The Beatles make their first US appearance
- Tokyo Olympics open

1965
- Courreges introduces the mini skirt in his '65 spring/summer haute couture line
- YSL introduces "Mondrian" dress
- Op-art/Pop Art influence on fashion
- US Air Force conducts first air strike on the North Vietnam
- Signing of Treaty on Basic Relations between Japan and the Republic of Korea

23

Beach bunny

A beach bag with another slant—snap it open, it's a straw mat that's big enough for you and a friend. Snap it shut, it's a tote with nine compartments to carry all your gear to and from the beach. Inflate two outside plastic pockets into pillows.

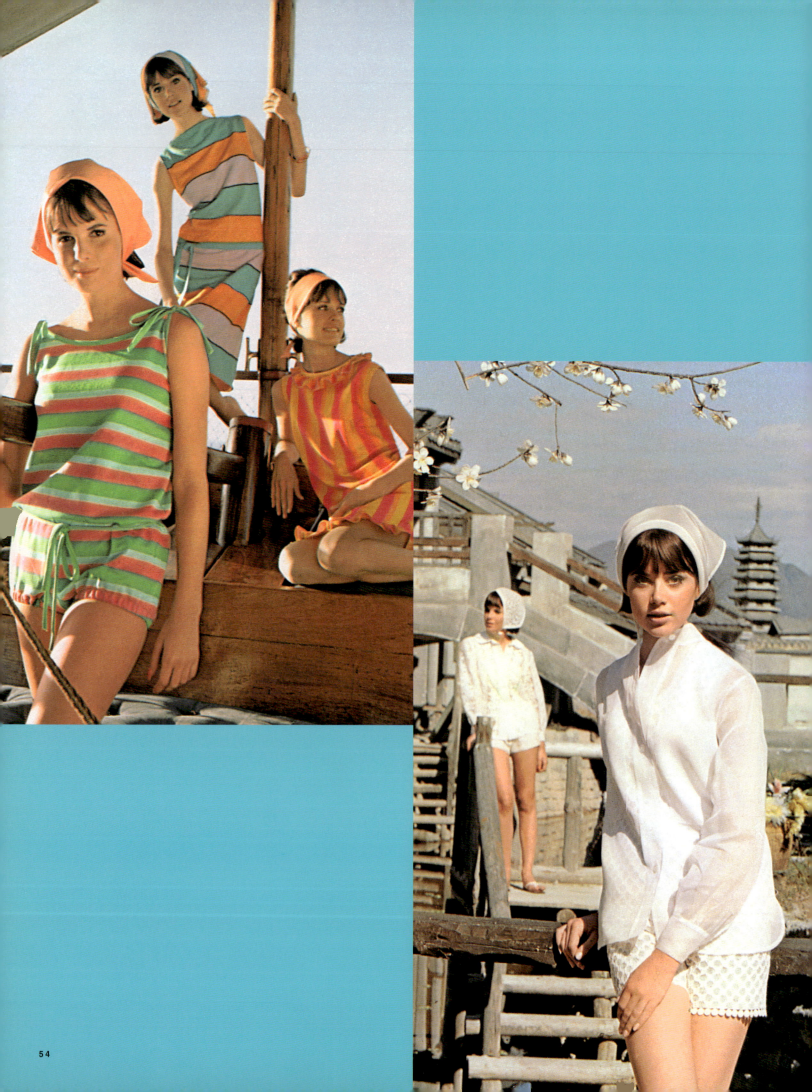

57

Popsicle brignts

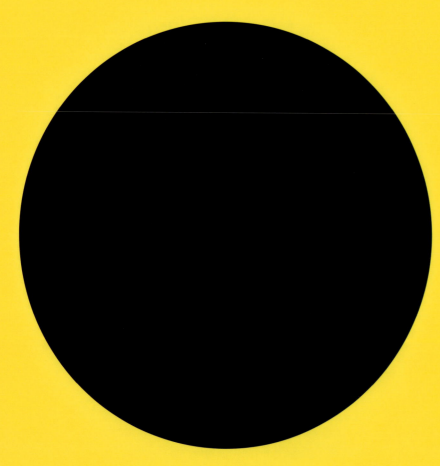

World traveler

103

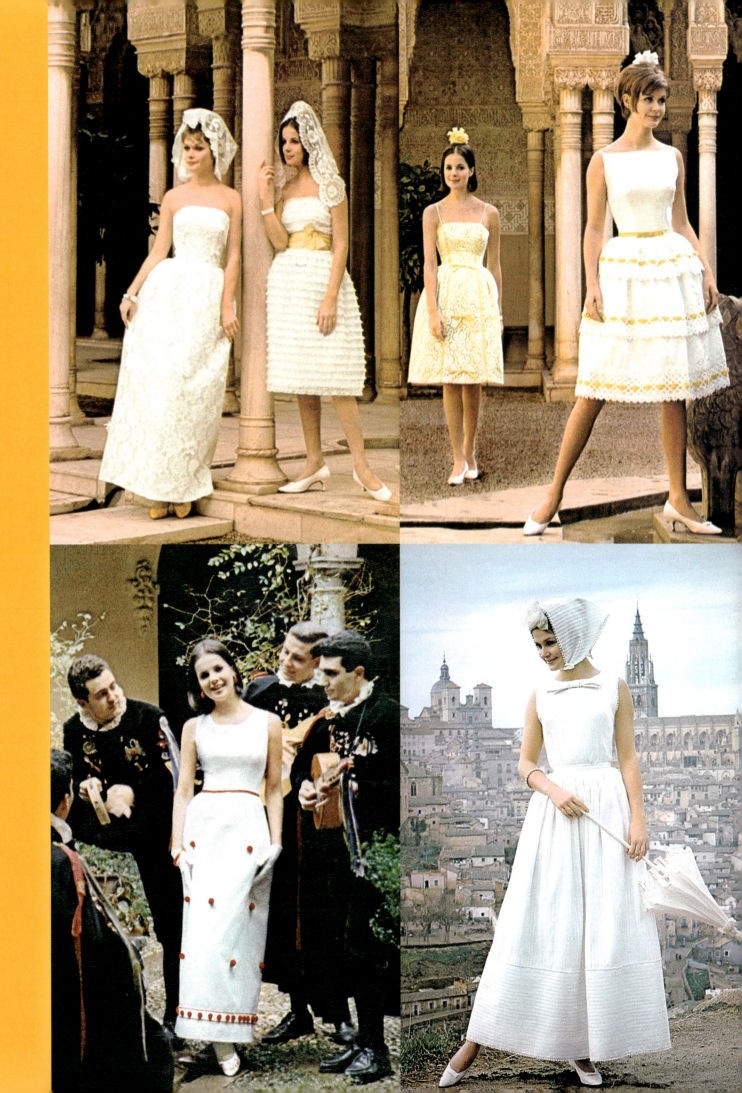

Sophisticates

winter

Coats

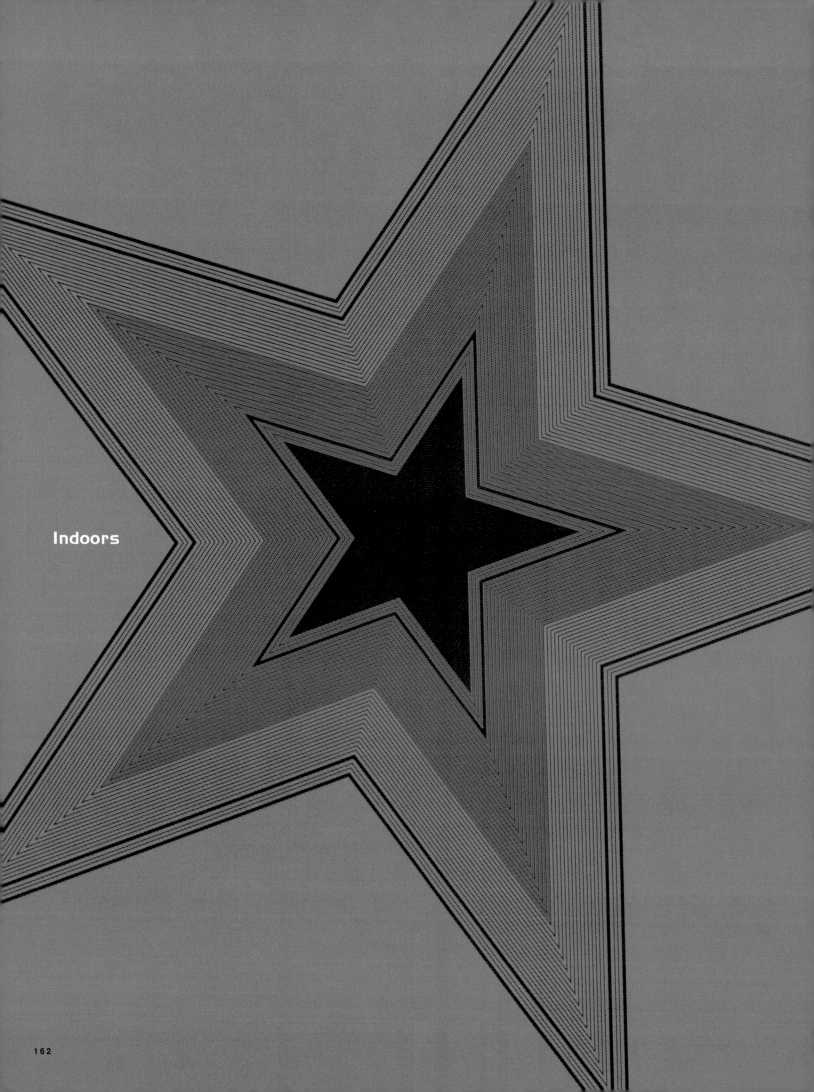
Indoors

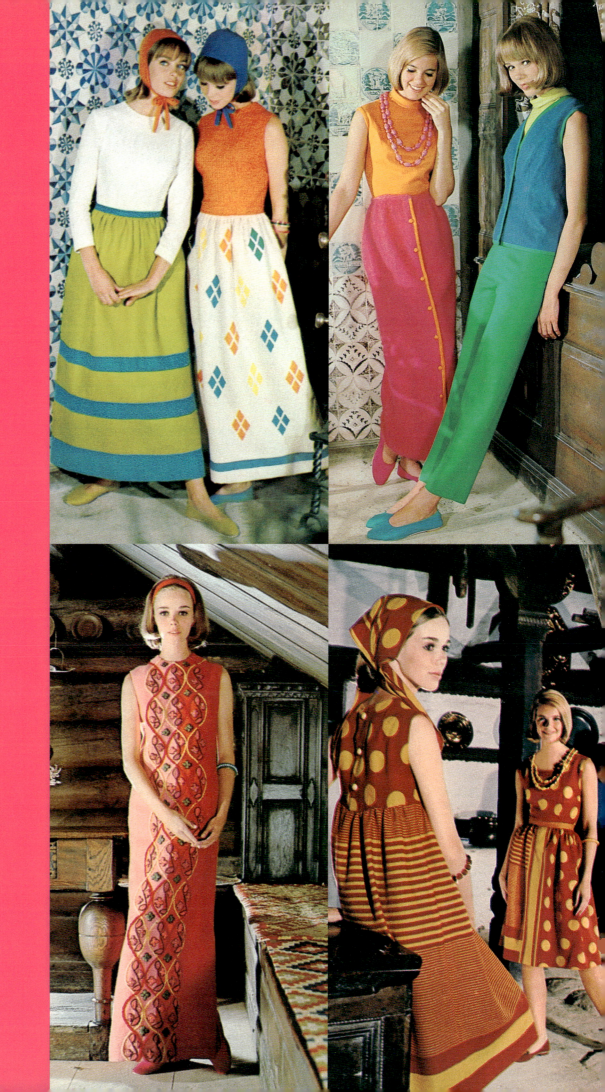

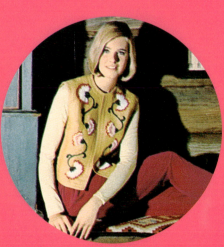

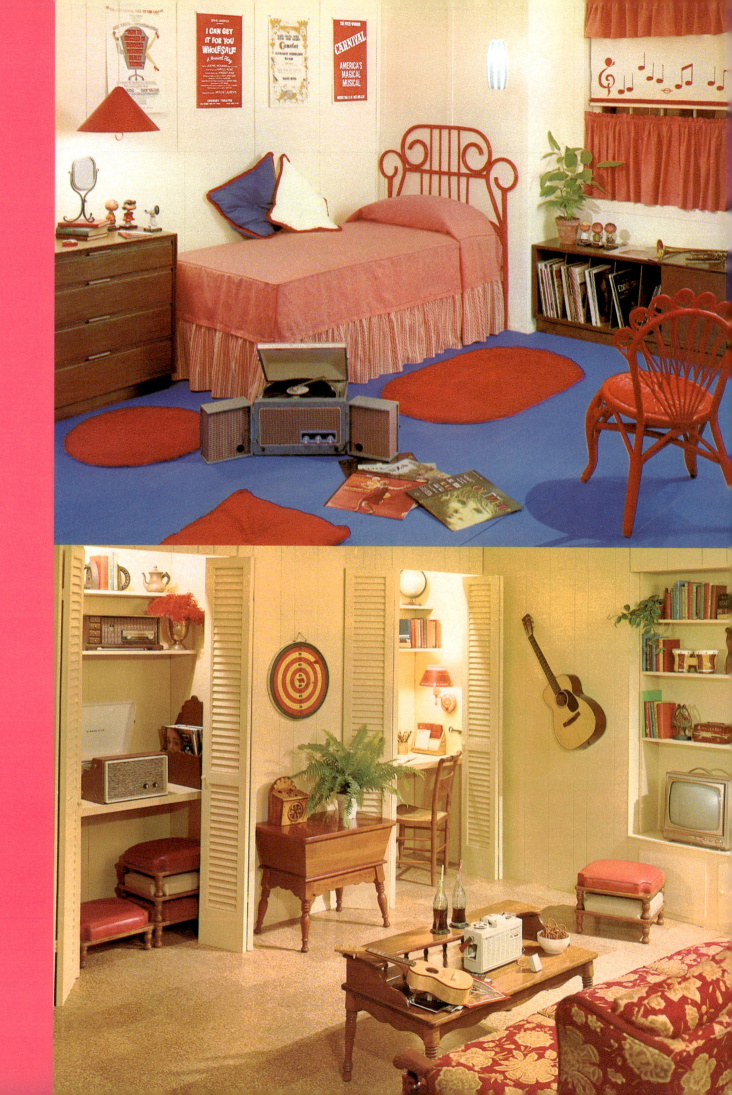

Hairdos

Holi-date Hairdos

Pick a pretty party set, comb it out casually for next-day sports

189

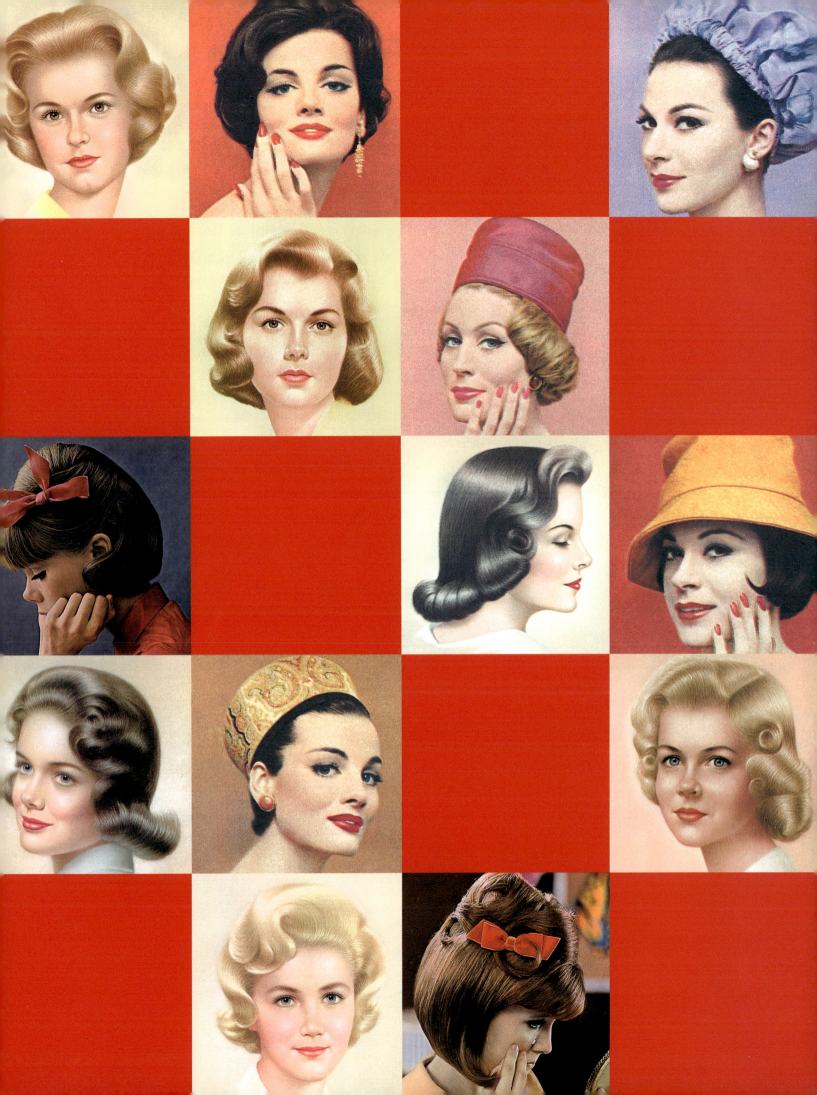

Shoes

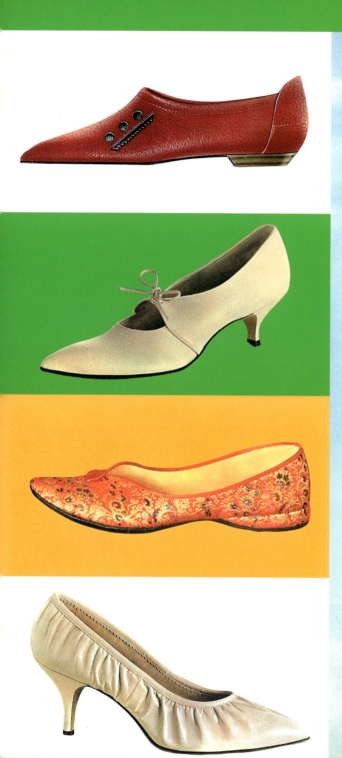

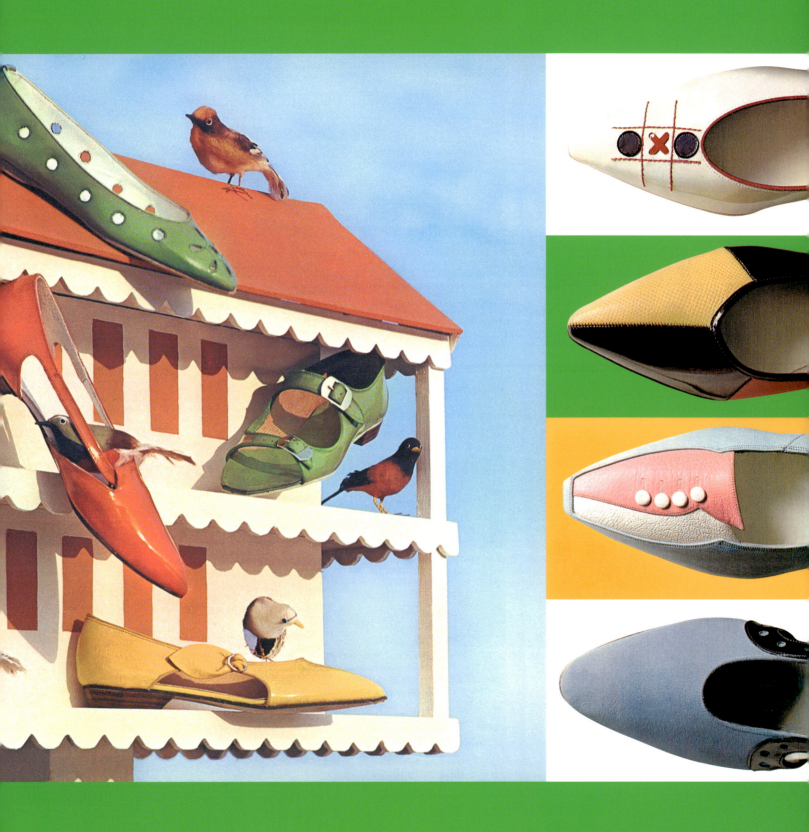

199

COLOR cues the patchwork news

Now is the time for all good flats to come to the aid of their colors! How? By adding one contrast to another, for new patchwork patterns in pastels or brights, fun to wear with solid-color clothes.

1. Textured, bone-toned leather brightens the vamp with insets of red, blue, lime, yellow, pink and orange.
2. Half white, half pink, with blue in view at the patchwork vamp. Textured leather, to wear with—white, pink, blue!
3. How to get a boot out of color: try this, of pastel suede in pistachio, pink, gold and blue mist, piped and laced with blue.
4. Skimmer of finely shirred kid, patched in six pretty pastels: yellow, salmon, green, blue, white and pink.
5. Sherbet shell: white plus DuPont's gleamy Pattina in orange and lemon.
6. Patchwork news for a suede tie-on: apricot, yellow, pink and green, to wear with pants pair-ups in any of these.
7. Bright flash here, to light up clothes in the pink-yellow-apricot range: a canvas slip-on, easy to wash, easy to pack.
8. Multicolor mix in textured leather, playing pale green against vivid orange and yellow. The flat heel is stacked.

Sneakers are the snazziest!

Step knee-deep in daisies or wear your heart in a brand-new place—on your knee socks! These are toasty-warm ones of Orlon and stretch nylon in a host of bright or neutral colors: red, gold, royal blue, black, tan, green, to name a few. The pierced heart and the long-stemmed daisy are appliqués of contrasting yarn; the cuffs are laced.

EARLY 60's FASHION STYLE
アーリー60's ファッションスタイル

2003年12月12日 初版第1刷発行

装丁・構成	大友 明子
編 集	高橋 かおる
発 行 人	三芳 伸吾
発 行 所	ピエ・ブックス

〒170-0005 東京都豊島区南大塚2-32-4
編集：TEL(03)5395-4820　FAX(03)5395-4821
　　　 e-mail:editor@piebooks.com
営業：TEL(03)5395-4811　FAX(03)5395-4812
　　　 e-mail:sales@piebooks.com
　　　 http://www.piebooks.com

印刷・製本　　株式会社サンニチ印刷

ご協力のお願い
今回の書籍出版にあたり調査をしましたが、最終的に連絡をとることができなかった写真家、モデルの方がいらっしゃいます。どなたか連絡先をご存じの方がいらっしゃいましたら、お手数ですが小社編集部までご一報下さい。

Please help…
Despite exhaustive investigation in preparing this book, there are still some photographers and models that we have been unable to contact. We ask anyone who knows how to contact these people to please notify our editorial staff, and thank you in advance for your assistance.

Copyright©2003 PIE BOOKS
Printed in Japan
ISBN4-89444-306-6 C0070

本書の収録内容の無断転載、複写、引用などを禁じます。
落丁、乱丁はお取り替えいたします。